A Polar Bear Biologist at Work

Dorothy Hinshaw Patent

A Wildlife Conservation Society Book

Franklin Watts
A Division of Scholastic Inc.
New York • Toronto • London • Auckland • Sydney
Mexico City • New Delhi • Hong Kong
Danbury, Connecticut

For Chuck

Library of Congress Cataloging-in-Publication Data

Patent, Dorothy Hinshaw.
A polar bear biologist at work / Dorothy Hinshaw Patent.
    p. cm.– (A Wildlife Conservation Society Book)
    Includes bibliographical references and index.
    Summary: Describes the work of Charles Jonkel, a biologist who studied polar bears in the Arctic and primarily in Churchill, Manitoba.
    ISBN 0-531-11850-9 (lib. bdg.)   0-531-16569-8 (pbk.)
    1. Polar bears—Research—Juvenile literature. 2. Jonkel, Chuck, 1930-
—Juvenile literature. [1. Polar bear. 2. Bears. 3. Jonkel, Charles, 1930- 4. Zoologists.]
I. Title.
QL737.C27 P3624   2001
59.786–dc21   00-038151

Contents

Meet the Author 4

Chapter 1   **An Accidental Discovery**...9

Chapter 2   **A Life Full of Bears**...13

Chapter 3   **The Polar Bears of Churchill** 19

Chapter 4   **A Polar Bear's Life**...27

Chapter 5   **Sharing the Planet with Bears**..................................37

Chapter 6   **A New Career** 43

Important Words 45

To Find Out More 46

Index 48

Meet the Author

Dorothy Hinshaw Patent has been writing about science and nature for children since 1972. She has written more than 100 books. Dorothy was born in Minnesota and grew up in California.

Dorothy has loved animals from the time she was a girl and studied biology at Stanford University,

Dorothy likes to experience what she writes about firsthand. Here, she holds a captive red wolf puppy while researching her book, Gray Wolf, Red Wolf.

Polar bears are perfectly adapted to life in a world of ice and snow.

where she earned a B.A. Then she received an M.A. and a Ph.D. from the University of California, Berkeley. She now lives in Missoula, Montana, with her husband and two dogs. She has two grown sons.

"I've been fascinated by bears for many years," says Dorothy. "I wrote my first book about them in 1979. Later on, I traveled to Alaska to observe grizzly bears. I find all bears interesting, but the polar bear has always seemed to be one of the most amazing animals on Earth. It lives in such a harsh climate, yet it thrives there.

"I've known Chuck Jonkel for many years and have always admired his knowledge of bears and his devotion to educating people about them. For years, I had wanted to join the group he leads every year to Churchill, a town in the Canadian province of Manitoba. During the trip, the group observes and learns all about polar bears. Finally, in 1995, I was able to go. Seeing polar bears up close and experiencing a little of their environment made me respect them even more.

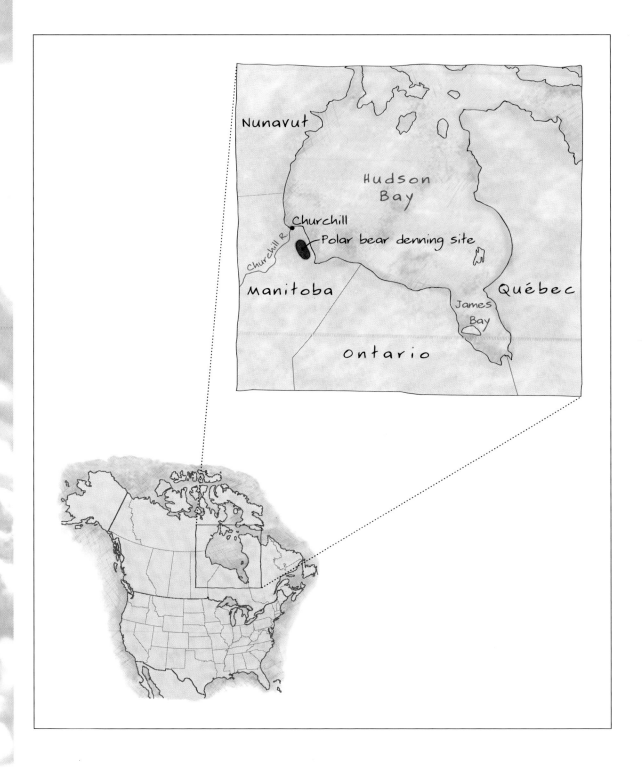

Chuck Jonkel loves the Arctic. Other people may wear hoods and hats to keep warm, but Chuck lets the cold wind rumple his hair.

"When the opportunity came to write this book, I was delighted by the chance to tell children about Chuck and his pioneering work with polar bears. I hope his story will inspire readers to pursue their own dreams and interests as they grow up."

Dorothy has received numerous awards and honors for her work, including the Eva Gordon Award from the American Nature Study Society and the Golden Kite from the Society of Children's Book Writers and Illustrators. You can learn more about Dorothy and her work by visiting her Web site at *www.dorothyhinshawpatent.com.*

This polar bear is running away from a helicopter.

An Accidental Discovery

One day in 1968, polar bear researcher Chuck Jonkel and a coworker were flying by helicopter across the barren northland of Canada. As they watched the ground pass below them, they noticed something strange.

"We began to see a lot of giant blocks of peat and a whole bunch of big holes in the banks of small lakes," Chuck says. "We saw pits that looked like giant birds' nests. What could they be?

"Then we saw a polar bear, and we knew the pits were their dens. We told the pilot to land. We spent the rest of the day looking at those dens, measuring them, crawling into them. There were polar bears all around—big old males sleeping in dens, females with cubs. Some of them were all blue in front, stained from the blueberries and crowberries they'd been eating. It was a fantastic place! Hundreds of bears and bear dens. Bears were swimming in the lakes and peeking out of their dens.

Scientists examine a polar bear den.

"The native people knew about this place, but didn't tell anybody else. The area is about 100 miles [161 kilometers] long and 30 miles [48 km] wide. It's the third, maybe even the second-biggest polar-bear-denning area in the world. About 200 cubs are born there every year."

Chuck was lucky to find this denning area. The scientists' helicopter was low on fuel, so they had decided to take a shortcut. If they had flown along their normal route, they would never have spotted the dens. Science is often like that. You can find something important when you least expect it.

The Way of the Bear

For thousands of years, polar bears have roamed the Arctic. Only native peoples knew where they lived and understood their way of life. They knew how polar bears hunt ringed seals, waiting patiently beside the seals' breathing holes in the ice until they come to the surface for air. They knew that pregnant female bears dig winter dens in the snow and then give birth to their cubs. They knew that the bears roam around the ice in all but the worst arctic blizzards. The native people showed their bravery and skill by hunting polar bears and killing them with spears and knives. Trying to kill a polar bear is dangerous. One swipe of a polar bear's paw can kill a seal, a dog, or a human hunter.

These Inuit polar bear hunters in the Canadian Arctic are using telescopes to spot their prey.

The American black bear lives in
forested areas of North America.

A Life Full of Bears

Chuck Jonkel knows all about both the good luck and the hard work that go into scientific research. He has been studying bears for more than 40 years. Chuck started to study black bears in 1959, while he was a student at the University of British Columbia in Canada. He began his polar bear research for the Canadian Wildlife Service in 1966.

"At first," Chuck says, "I knew how to work with bears, but I knew nothing about working in the Arctic. I stumbled around the Arctic, looking for polar bears.

Chuck Jonkel: The Facts	
DATE AND PLACE OF BIRTH: **July 16, 1930, Chicago, Illinois**	
FAMILY:	**Married to wife Joan, two grown children**
SCIENTIFIC TRAINING:	**Bachelor of Science degree, University of Montana; Master of Science degree, University of Montana; Doctor of Philosophy degree, University of British Columbia**
HOBBIES:	**Hiking, camping, gardening**

The arctic tundra seems to stretch endlessly in all directions.

I learned how easy it is to get lost on the *tundra*, where there are no trees or other landmarks. In the summer, the mosquitoes ate me alive. In the winter, the cold was terrible. I decided never to go outside in a strange place without an Inuit [Eskimo] along."

Chuck's work took him to many parts of Arctic Canada, Svalbard (a group of islands in the Arctic Ocean), and Greenland. He discovered that the best place to study polar bears was around Churchill, Manitoba, on Hudson Bay. Unlike most of the Canadian Arctic, Churchill was easy to reach. A branch of the railroad crossed the barren land and ended up in Churchill. There was also an airstrip that researchers could use, so the town made a good headquarters for polar bear research.

The International Wildlife Film Festival

In the late 1960s, Chuck began to worry about the lack of quality and accuracy in wildlife films. "One bad film could undo 10 years of work in educating the public about nature," he says. "This was particularly true for bears, but many kinds of animals suffered from the Hollywood and Disneyland treatments." He talked to his friend, Canadian wildlife film producer Jim Murray. The two men decided that a competition that judged wildlife films would improve the situation.

In the late 1970s, Chuck mentioned the idea to students in the Wildlife Club at the University of Montana. They were so enthusiastic that they created a film festival that now sets wildlife film standards worldwide. Each year, films are judged on their quality, their scientific accuracy, and their ability to promote learning and understanding about nature. About 10,000 people attend the annual film showings.

In the Arctic, ice called *permafrost* remains in the ground all year round. In northwest Greenland, the average temperature remains below freezing until July. The region around Hudson Bay in Canada has an arctic climate, even though it extends far south of the Arctic Circle. This is the most southern point where polar bears live in the wild.

In the early 1970s, Chuck began to look beyond his work in the Arctic. He enjoyed the research, but his home was in Ottawa, Ontario, the capital city of Canada. He and his wife, Joan, did not want their two children to grow up in a big, eastern city.

Chuck decided to look for another job. He found one at the University of Montana in Missoula, where he studies grizzly bears. But he never gave up his love for the Arctic and its polar bears.

About 1 million people live in Ottawa, Ontario—Canada's capital city.

Where Polar Bears Live

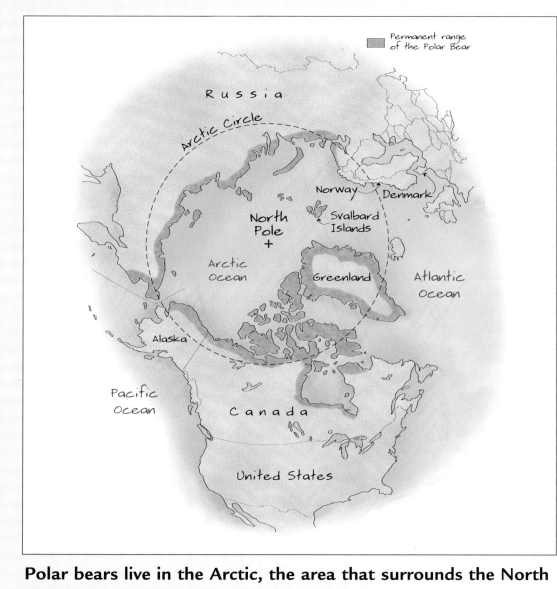

Permanent range of the Polar Bear

Russia

Arctic Circle

Norway   Denmark

North
Pole
+

Svalbard
Islands

Arctic
Ocean

Greenland   Atlantic
Ocean

Alaska

Pacific
Ocean

C a n a d a

United States

Polar bears live in the Arctic, the area that surrounds the North Pole. Its outer edge is the Arctic Circle—an imaginary line that you can see on any globe.

Life in the Arctic

On the first day of winter—the shortest day of the year—the sun doesn't even rise north of the Arctic Circle. At the North Pole, the sun never rises all winter long. The only light comes from a faint glow on the horizon and from the moon and the stars.

Starting in late December, the days begin to get longer. After the first day of spring, the days become longer the farther north you go. On the first day of summer—the longest day of the year—the sun doesn't set north of the Arctic Circle. It is bright and sunny all day and all night.

During the arctic winter, the sun rises late and sets early.

The Polar Bears of Churchill

Once Chuck decided to do research in Churchill, he quickly figured out how to work with polar bears. It took courage, though. "I had to go through a learn-ing period," he says.

"When I took the job, three people who knew about polar bears all told me the same thing. They'd put an arm over my shoulder and say, 'Son, those polar bears hunt you all the time.' I began to wonder what I was getting myself into.

Luckily for me, those people were wrong. Polar bears are actually quite a bit easier to work with than grizzly bears or black bears. They don't get upset by people. Sometimes they even fall asleep while you're watching."

The polar bears that live around Hudson Bay have a unique lifestyle. They are the only polar bears in the world that spend many months each year on land. When the ice on the bay melts in July, the bears come ashore.

As long as there is ice on Hudson Bay, polar bears can hunt for seals. But when the ice melts, they come on shore.

When Chuck began his studies, scientists didn't know where the bears traveled. He found that after spending the summer along the shoreline and farther inland, they gathered along the shores of Cape Churchill every autumn, waiting for the ice to form. Dozens of bears were often present at the same time, making them easy to study.

Learning About Bears

Working with the bears meant first trapping them. Chuck would build a V-shaped structure out of driftwood and rocks. He placed some tasty bait at the back of the V. Next, he set a foot snare—a trap that would catch the bear's foot—at the entrance of the structure. Chuck attached the snare to a 50-gallon (189-liter) barrel full of sand and rocks. This would make it impossible for the polar bear to run away.

Finally, he put "stepping sticks" around the snare's loop and trigger to guide the bear's steps.

Chuck checked the traps twice each day. When he found a bear, he used a dart gun to inject a *tranquilizer* into the animal. The tranquilizer made the bear fall asleep so that Chuck could handle it. He measured and weighed the animal and took a blood sample. Then he pulled a tooth to determine the animal's age.

Chuck and another scientist remove a tooth from a tranquilized polar bear.

Each bear got an ear tag and a tattooed number so that it could be recognized later.

Over the years, Chuck and other researchers have learned a lot about the Churchill bears. While they are on land, the bear population splits up. The big males take the best *habitat* along the coast. The coast makes a good home for the bears because they can easily dig holes in the sand and lie there to keep cool. They can cool off by taking a dip in the bay too. The bay also provides them with some food. The dominant females and the other adult males live a bit farther inland. Young males and the younger females with cubs live farthest inland.

A female bear and her cubs rest outside their den entrance inland from Hudson Bay.

Polar bears are comfortable swimming in frigid arctic water.

During the summer, many of the females and their young visit the denning area that Chuck discovered. They dig down to the permafrost to stay cool. In some years, they eat a lot of berries, grasses, and sedges, like their grizzly bear relatives. They also eat kelp, or seaweed, and mussels as well as other sea creatures that wash ashore.

This is not enough food to nourish their huge bodies, but they have ways of solving the food-supply problem. They enter a resting state similar to the winter *hibernation* of other bears. Some scientists call this state "walking hibernation." During walking hibernation, the bears' bodies recycle the chemicals they need over and over again. They use up less fat than they normally would. This helps them survive and stay strong on little or no food.

Polar bears wait along the shore of the Hudson Bay for ice to form.

Waiting for the Ice

In the autumn, the polar bears gather in the Churchill area. They somehow know that the ice forms first on Cape Churchill. Freshwater freezes at a warmer temperature than seawater, so it ices up earlier. Freshwater ice comes down the Seal River and the Churchill River. The northwest wind blows the floating pieces of ice toward the Cape, where they pile up and form the first ice shelf of the season. Then the hungry bears leave the land and return to the Arctic ice to hunt seals.

Living with Bears in Churchill

When the bears gather near the town of Churchill in the autumn, they can cause trouble. Polar bears don't usually attack humans, but they are not afraid of people. If a bear feels threatened and cannot escape, it may attack.

The people of Churchill have made efforts to learn to live with the bears. The Polar Bear Alert program teaches people how to avoid trouble with bears. Traps are set to catch any bears wandering in or near the town. These bears are kept in a special building called "bear jail" until the ice forms. If people see a polar bear in town, they call the Polar Bear Alert number: 675-BEAR. The bear is either chased out of town or trapped and taken to the bear jail.

When polar bears get in trouble at Churchill, they are tranquilized and put in "bear jail" until the ice forms. In the jail they are given water but no food.

The thick fluffy coats of these wrestling polar bears protect them from the cold.

A Polar Bear's Life

Over the years, scientists have learned a great deal about how polar bears live. Most of them spend their entire lives on the arctic ice and snow. They are perfectly adapted to this environment. A polar bear's thick coat has two layers. Dense, soft underfur lies against the bear's black skin. Mixed with the underfur are longer, coarser *guard hairs* that soak up heat from the sun.

Pockets of air trapped in the thick underfur are held in place by the guard hairs. The air holds in warmth. A thick layer of fat, called *blubber*, under the skin also helps keep the bear warm, especially when it swims. The blubber layer is 2 to 4 inches (5 to 10 cm) thick.

A polar bear's feet are as big as dinner plates. They allow the bear to walk on soft snow without sinking in. The bottoms of the feet are covered with fur, keeping the bear's feet warm. The fur also keeps the bear's feet from sliding on slippery ice and snow.

The polar bear's big, furry feet act like snowshoes, supporting their bodies as they walk across the snow.

A polar bear can swim for 20 miles (32 km) through water cold enough to kill a person in just a few minutes. The bear holds its back legs together and uses them as a rudder while paddling with its front feet. The front toes are partly webbed, which makes swimming easier.

Varieties of Polar Bears

Scientists think the polar bear developed from the brown bear in the Pacific Ocean area of the Arctic 250,000 to 100,000 years ago. Today, polar bears that live in different areas look different from one another. Those closest to Siberia, in Russia, and in northern Alaska look most like brown bears.

Polar bears on the opposite side of the North Pole, around Svalbard, have longer necks and wedge-shaped bodies. Their longer neck makes it easier for the bears to breathe while swimming. Their wedge-shaped body cuts through the water well. These bears seem to be more highly adapted to life in the water. They are also smaller than the coastal Alaskan and Siberian bears.

Scientists believe that the ancestors of brown bears (top) are also the ancestors of polar bears (bottom).

The Great Seal Hunter

By far the most important item in a polar bear's diet is the ringed seal, the most common seal in the Arctic. These seals spend most of their time under the arctic ice, hunting for food, such as fish and shrimp. They come up for air at breathing holes that they keep open with their claws and teeth.

Each seal has a number of breathing holes. Polar bears use their keen sense of smell to find the seals' breathing holes. A bear may wait for hours for a

Ringed seals spend their entire lives on and around the arctic ice. A ringed seal can stay underwater for an hour or more without breathing.

A patient polar bear flattens itself on the ice as it waits by a ringed seal's breathing hole.

seal. When the seal surfaces, the bear strikes it with a front paw. It hooks the seal with its sharp claws, and then grabs it with its teeth. A polar bear can pull a 200-pound (91-kilogram) seal through the breathing hole in one swift movement, crushing the bones in the seal's body.

The easiest hunting is from mid-March to early June, when ringed seal pups are young. When a female ringed seal gives birth, she leaves the pup under a protective shell of ice and snow called an *aglu* (AG-loo). For the first 2 weeks of life, a seal pup can't go into the water, making it perfect polar bear food. When a bear locates an aglu, it approaches quietly. Then suddenly, it pounces, breaking through the top and grabbing the seal pup with its sharp claws. If the female seal returns to protect the pup, the bear may get an extra meal.

The seals are also easy to hunt when they lie on the ice. A polar bear will sneak up on a group of seals very slowly—then pounce on one of them.

A polar bear usually eats the skin and thick blubber layer of its *prey* and leaves the meat behind for other animals, such as arctic foxes. Half the weight of an older ringed seal pup can be fat, so it provides the bear with a generous meal. Besides, digesting meat requires a lot of freshwater, and there is no liquid freshwater on the arctic ice. Melting the cold snow in its mouth could use up more energy than the meat provides. Digesting fat, however, releases water. Fat also contains much more energy than the protein in meat.

Polar bears may also eat fish and birds, such as geese. They nibble on grasses, consume mussels and seaweed, and forage for berries in autumn. Occasionally, they eat

These Churchill bears are digging for a snack of seaweed called kelp.

goose eggs or dead caribou, musk oxen—or even other polar bears. Nonetheless, ringed seals remain their main food item. A big polar bear can put on 300 to 500 pounds (136 to 227 kg) of fat during the few months ringed seals are easy prey.

Having a Family

Polar bears begin to have young when they are 5 to 6 years old. After mating, the male and female go their separate ways. The female usually gives birth to one to three tiny cubs in a winter den. Rarely, four cubs are born.

Polar Bears: The Facts

SCIENTIFIC NAME:	*Ursus maritimus* (Latin for "sea-going bear")
FOOD:	Mostly ringed seals, also dead caribou, musk oxen, and other animals; sometimes fish, berries, kelp, mussels, and other foods
BODY LENGTH:	6 1/2 to 8 feet (2 to 2.5 m)
WEIGHT:	Males 990 to 1760 pounds (450 to 800 kg); females 495 to 990 pounds (224 to 450 kg)
SPEED ON LAND:	Bursts of up to 19 miles (30 km) per hour
SWIMMING SPEED:	About 4 miles (6.5 km) per hour
LIFESPAN:	45 years in captivity, 30 in the wild; most live no more than 18 years
LOCATION:	The arctic region; mostly around the North Pole
POPULATION:	Estimated at 21,000 to 28,500 worldwide

The newborn cubs are almost naked and can neither hear nor see. Each cub weighs less than 2 pounds (900 grams), but it grows fast on its mother's rich milk. While cow's milk has less than 4 percent fat, polar-bear milk has more than 30 percent fat.

By the time they are 2 months old, polar bear cubs can hear and see, and their bodies are covered by thick, soft fur. The den is big enough for them to wander around and play together, strengthening their muscles for life in the challenging Arctic.

The mother and cubs leave the den in early spring at about the same time the ringed seals give birth. Each cub is now about the size of a cocker spaniel. After a few days of getting used to life outside the den, the cubs follow their mother onto the ice.

Bear cubs learn how to survive from their mothers. They carefully observe how she hunts and how she makes a den in the ice and snow. The female also protects her cubs from large male bears—their only enemies besides humans. By the time the cubs are 2 years old, they can take care of themselves and are ready to leave their mother. If they haven't been able to feed well, they may stay with her longer. A wild polar bear can live to be 30 years old, but this is rare.

As polar bear cubs grow, their mother teaches them many important things, such as how to hunt and where to dig a den.

Years ago, polar bears like this one could easily feed in the open dumps at Churchill. Now, there is only one dump, and the bears are kept away.

Sharing the Planet with Bears

Chapter 5

Humans now live on every continent on Earth.
Everywhere we go, we make demands on the environment. People destroy the habitats of plants and animals by cutting down forests and building houses, shopping malls, and cities. In the Arctic, human activities are more limited, but they still cause problems for the creatures that live there. Fortunately, people care enough about polar bears to want to help them survive.

Protecting Polar Bears

In the early 1960s, Russia became concerned about the survival of polar bears and wanted a temporary ban on hunting them. "The Russian bears had been hurt terribly during World War II," Chuck explains. "Leningrad and Moscow were blockaded by the Nazis. No food or other goods could get in or out, so the supply lines to people living in the Arctic closed down. They needed to hunt to eat. A lot of people lived off the land, which meant shooting anything they could and eating it. They killed a huge number of bears."

At that time, many scientists believed that polar bears travel long distances. They believed the same bear could show up in Russia, Alaska, Canada, or Greenland. The Russians thought that if polar bears were protected everywhere, it would help the Russian bears recover. The United States agreed with Russia, but Canada was against the hunting ban. Canada had lots of bears. Besides, many native people in Canada still hunted polar bears for food, clothing, and trade.

"I believed that polar bears tend to stay in one area, not roam all over the Arctic," Chuck explains. "I felt that the bears should be managed on that basis. Banning hunting in Canada wouldn't help the Russian bears recover. To back up my theory, I had to find boundaries for areas where the bears lived.

Polar bears are still important to native people such as the Inuk on Ellesmere Island, Canada. This hunter is wearing polar bear pants.

The Churchill polar bears, like these two sparring bears, spend their entire lives in the James Bay area.

"I drew lines on a map, based on what I knew. I had very little information to work with, but I figured the bears wouldn't cross the open ocean or mountains like those running up the middle of Greenland. I believed that the bears in the James Bay area of Canada stayed there. The Churchill bears stayed in their area, and the other bears did likewise," he says.

Chuck worked with other scientists to set up the Polar Bear Specialist Group for the International Union for Conservation of Nature (IUCN). The group helped get the polar bear nations to agree on a plan. Russia and Norway would protect their bears completely, while Canada, Denmark, and the United States would allow hunting only by native people who live in the polar bear areas. All the nations agreed to cooperate in studying polar bears and in protecting their habitats. Luckily, Chuck's theory about where the bears live was correct. Later studies showed that the lines he drew were accurate.

Dangers to Bears

While polar bears do not seem to be decreasing in numbers now, the future holds many dangers. Arctic oil drilling is a major problem for the bears. One big oil spill could poison the feeding and denning sites of hundreds of polar bears. They would also die from licking the toxic oil off their fur. The oil would darken the ice, making it soak up heat and melt. The same danger exists wherever oil is shipped or where drilling takes place in the Arctic.

Recently, global warming has become perhaps the biggest danger to arctic wildlife. Several new studies show that polar ice is melting and thinning rapidly. As Chuck explains, "The ice on Hudson Bay is breaking up earlier than it used to near Churchill. That means the bears go out later in the autumn and come off the ice earlier in the spring.

The ice on Hudson Bay starts out as pieces that then freeze together to make a solid surface.

They lose 2 weeks of hunting in the autumn and then another 2 weeks in the spring. They have much less time to feed, which can't be good for the bears."

The polar bears around Hudson Bay will probably be the first to disappear if this warming process continues, because they already live on the southern edge of polar bear habitat. It would be a great loss if these bears—so perfectly adapted to the arctic environment—disappear forever because we destroyed their only homeland.

A polar bear cub is secure under the protection of its powerful mother.

A New Career

Chuck has changed his career many times since leaving Canada. But polar bears are still an important part of his life, and Churchill is still one of his favorite places. Every year, he leads groups of students and travelers there to experience and learn about the Arctic. The most popular course takes place at the end of October, when the polar bears are gathering to wait for the ice to form on Hudson Bay.

On these trips, Chuck teaches people not only about polar bears, but also about the world of the Arctic. They learn about the lives of other arctic animals, such as caribou, and birds called

Chuck Jonkel, on the far right, explains how a polar bear trap is set.

ptarmigan. Chuck digs into the ground so that his students can feel the permafrost. They also learn about the geography of the Arctic.

Chuck takes his students to the schools in Churchill, where they meet with children and give talks. He helps people from many places connect with one another. The main focus, however, is always the bears.

"For a lot of people, experiencing the Arctic literally changes their lives," says Chuck. "They become more caring, and they look at things from the viewpoint of other animals and other people. Bears are great for teaching people about nature."

People love polar bears, making them good ambassadors for all arctic wildlife.

Important Words

aglu   (noun) a shell of snow and ice made by a mother seal to protect her pup

blubber   (noun) a thick layer of fat under the skin

guard hairs   (noun) long, hollow hairs that help insulate animals from the cold

habitat   (noun) the place where a plant, animal, or any other creature normally lives

hibernation   (noun) resting in a protected place during the winter, usually without eating

permafrost   (noun) permanently frozen ground found under the arctic tundra

prey   (noun) an animal that is hunted and killed for food by another animal

tranquilizer   (noun) a drug used to calm an animal or make it fall asleep

tundra   (noun) treeless land found in polar regions

To Find Out More

Books and Magazine Articles

Drew, Lisa. "Tales of the Great White Bear." *National Wildlife* (December/January 1997), 16–25.

Lynch, Wayne. "Den Mothers and Their Cubs." *International Wildlife*. (November/December 1994), 12–17.

Miller, Debbie S. *A Polar Bear Journey*. Boston: Little, Brown and Company, 1997.

Patent, Dorothy Hinshaw. *Great Ice Bear, The Polar Bear and the Eskimo*. New York: Morrow Junior Books, 1999.

_____. *Polar Bears*. Minneapolis, MN: Carolrhoda, 2000.

Stirling, Ian. *Bears*. San Francisco, CA: Sierra Club Books for Children, 1992.

Videos

Arctic Kingdom: Life at the Edge, National Geographic, 1996.

Polar Bear Alert, National Geographic, 1982.

Organizations and Online Sites

International Wildlife Film Festival
27 Fort Missoula Road, Suite 2
Missoula, MT 59804
www.Wildlifefilms.org
This Web site describes the winning films for the last few years, gives information about the next festival, and tells about other events. For example, filmmaking workshops for children may be offered during the summer.

The Last Roar of the White Bear
http://imp.uow.edu.au/staff/feen/polarbear/pbarticle1.html
This article discusses the problem of polar bear survival as polar ice melts.

Polar Bears Alive
http://polarbearsalive.org/
Polar Bears Alive is a nonprofit organization that protects polar bears and their habitat. Their Web site features facts about polar bears, photos, a store, and much more.

Sea World's Polar Bear Page
http://seaworld.org//polar_bears/pbindex.html
This Web site is packed with information about polar bears and how they live.

Wildlife Conservation Society
http://www.wcs.org
2300 Southern Blvd.
Bronx, NY 10460-1099

Index

Arctic, 11, 13, 16, 24, 29, 30, 34, 37, 38, 40, 43, 44
Arctic Circle, *17*, 18
Blubber, 27, 32
Canadian Wildlife Service, 13
Churchill, Manitoba, 5, 14, 19, 22, 24, 25, 39, 40, 43, 44
Claws, 30, 31
Cubs, 9, 10, 11, 22, *23*, 33, 34–35, *35*
Dangers to polar bears, 40–41
Dens, 9, 10, *10*, 11, *22*, 34, 35
    denning area, 10, 23, 40
Feet, 27, *28*
Food, 9, 23, 32, 33, *33*
Guard hairs, 27
Hudson Bay, 14, 16, 19, *20*, 22, *24*, 40, 41, *41*, 43
International Wildlife Film Festival, The, 15
Jonkel, Chuck, 5, 7, *7*, 9, 10, 13–16, 19–21, *21*, 22, 23, 37, 39, 40, 43, *43*, 44
Mating and birth, 33
Murray, Jim, 15
Native peoples, 10, 38, 40
    Inuit, *11*, 14

Inuk, *38*
North Pole, *17*, 18, 29
Ottawa, Ontario, 16, *16*
Patent, Dorothy Hinshaw, 4–7, *4*
Permafrost, 16, 23, 44
Polar Bear Alert program, 25
    bear jail, 25, *25*
Polar Bear Specialist Group, 39
Protecting polar bears, 37–40
    hunting ban, 37, 38
Range of polar bears, 16, *17*
Ringed seals, 11, 30, *30*, 31, 32, 33, 35
    aglu, 32
Scientists, 10, *10*, 20, *21*, 23, 27, 29, 38
Summer, 18, 20, 23
Swimming, *23*, 28
Teeth, 30, 31
Trapping polar bears, 21, 25
    ear tag, 22
    tattoo, 22
    tranquilizer, 21
Tundra, 14, *14*
Underfur, 27
Walking hibernation, 23
Winter, 18, *18*

Photographs © :Alaska Stock Images: 5, 20, 28 (Johnny Johnson), back cover, 9, 13, 19, 27, 37, 43, 45, 46; Dorothy H. Patent: 8, 10, 21 (Charles Jonkel), 22 (William Munoz), 41, 43; Eyewire: 15; Images of Nature/Thomas D. Mangelsen: 18, 23, 24, 35, 44; John Hawver: 39; Liaison Agency, Inc.: 25 (Figaro De Wildenberg), 16 (Andrew Klapatiuk); Mary Hawver: 7, 29 bottom; Mel Woods: 4; National Geographic Image Collection/ Norbert Rosing: 42; Peter Arnold Inc.: 11 (Fred Bruemmer), 26 (S. J. Krasemann); Photo Researchers, NY: 38 (B & C Alexander), cover, 36 (Dan Guravich), 31 (Stephen J. Krasemann), 29 top (Leonard Lee Rue III), 14 (Leonard Rue Jr.), 30 (Simon); Photodisc, Inc.: border art, 1; Visuals Unlimited/Tom Walker: 12; Wolfgang Käehler/Provia: 33. Maps by XNR Productions, Inc.